D1245365

One Day at a Time

*A Collection of Quotes to Lift You
Up and Carry You Through*

Curated by
John Sequeira

Copyright © John Sequeira 2020

All rights reserved. No part of this publication
may be reproduced, stored in a retrieval system, or
transmitted in any form or by any means, mechanical,
photocopying, recording or otherwise, without prior
permission in writing of the author.

ISBN: 9798563333567 (paperback)

"The quotes in this book have been drawn from dozens
of sources. They are assumed to be accurate as quoted in
their previously published forms. The publisher cannot
guarantee their perfect accuracy."

Table of Contents

Introduction

Almost ten years ago, I started collecting quotes that I read or were sent to me by friends and colleagues that touched and inspired me. This has been an especially difficult year and one we will likely never forgot. I found myself going back to my collection to pick me up and carry me through the darkest times.

I realized putting together a collection of what were the "best of the best" could help others for years to come. My hope is that these quotes give you joy, happiness and motivation in the same way they have carried me. Thanks to various authors that have placed their thoughts and wisdom into the public domain to help the human race be the best version of ourselves every day.

Starting every morning with a positive inspirational message can set the tone for a great and blessed day.

JANUARY

January 1

Constantly re-evaluate your lifetime plan.
If you fail to plan, you may inadvertently
be planning to fail.
Unknown

January 2

How exciting are your dreams? Most people don't aim too high and miss, they aim too low and hit.
Unknown

January 3

The mind is like water. When it's turbulent,
it's difficult to see. When it's calm,
everything becomes clear.
Buddha

January 4

The wonderful thing about the game of life is that winning and losing are only temporary – unless you quit.
Unknown

January 5

Every thought is a seed. If you plant crab apples, don't count on harvesting Golden Delicious.
Unknown

January 6

*Once the human mind is stretched by a new
idea, it will never again return
to its original size.
By Oliver Wendell Holmes*

January 7

Carry out a random act of kindness, with no expectation of reward, safe in the knowledge that one day someone might do the same for you.
Princess Diana

January 8

It's not what happens to you that count, but how you handle it. It's not how far you fall, but how well you bounce.
Unknown

January 9

The smallest goal achieved stands taller than the grandest intention. Do whatever your heart leads you to do – but do it.
Unknown

January 10

What went wrong-This is a story of four people, Everybody, Somebody, Anybody and Nobody. There was an important job to be done and everybody was sure that somebody would do it. Anybody could have done it but nobody did it. Somebody got angry because it was everybody's job. Everybody thought that somebody would do it but nobody asked anybody. It ended up that the job wasn't done and everybody blamed somebody, when actually nobody asked anybody.
Unknown

January 11

*Where I put my time is
where I put my life.
Unknown*

January 12

Understanding is an art. And not everyone is an artist.
Buddha

January 13

*I will never have total agreement
with everyone about everything but
disagreement does not dictate that
I have to be disagreeable.*
Unknown

January 14

Help me to live with the confidence that what I need to meet life's challenges you will provide at the right time.
Sue Monk Kidd

January 15

Don't waste words on people who deserve your silence. Sometimes the most powerful thing you can say is nothing at all.
Unknown

January 16

Don't practice till you get it right, practice till you can't get it wrong.
McKayla Maroney

January 17

*Stop waiting for others to change. Ask
yourself why others should be different
simply because you would like it better if
they were. Recognize that every person has
a right to be whatever they choose, even if
you irritate yourself about it.*
Wayne Dyer

January 18

We are all writing the story of our lives.
Are you satisfied with the script so far?
Matthew Kelly

January 19

The ultimate measure of a man is not where he stands in moments of comfort and convenience, but where he stands at times of challenge and controversy.
Martin Luther King Jr.

January 20

If you want to go quickly, go alone.
If you want to go far, go together.
African Proverb

January 21

*If you focus on the hurt you will continue
to suffer, however if you focus on the lesson
you will continue to grow.*
Buddha

January 22

Integrity is choosing courage over comfort;
it's choosing what's right over what's fun,
fast or easy; and it's practicing your values,
not just professing them.
Brene Brown

January 23

*I never judge anyone because it doesn't
allow me the time to love them.
Mother Teresa*

John Sequeira

January 24

When faced with our human imperfection, we can either respond with kindness and care or with judgment and criticism.
Kristin Neff

January 25

As you climb the ladder of success, check occasionally to make sure it is leaning against the right wall.
Unknown

January 26

*The happiest of people don't necessarily
have the best of everything; they just make
the most of everything they have.
Unknown*

January 27

When you rise in the morning, think of what a precious privilege it is to be alive, to breathe, to think, to enjoy, and to love.
Marcus Aurelius

January 28

You are braver then you believe, stronger than you seem, smarter than you think and more loved than you know.
Unknown

January 29

Humility is the pathway to knowledge.
Fulton Sheen

January 30

Not everything that is faced can be changed; but nothing can be changed until it is faced.
James Baldwin

January 31

Life is a daring adventure or nothing at all.
Helen Keller

FEBRUARY

February 1

Shame needs three things to grow – secrecy, silence and judgement.
Brene Brown

February 2

Stop trying to make everybody happy.
You're not tequila.
Unknown

February 3

Quiet the mind and the soul will speak.
Buddha

February 4

It's better to walk alone than to be walking with a crowd going in the wrong direction.
Unknown

February 5

*Forgiveness does not change the past
but it does enlarge the future.*
Unknown

February 6

*Why do we only rest in peace? Why don't
we live in peace too?*
Unknown

February 7

You miss 100% of the shots you don't take.
Wayne Gretzky

February 8

*Every moment of every day, every
situation, every person we encounter is an
opportunity to become a better
version of ourselves.*
Matthew Kelly

February 9

Ability may get you to the top, but it takes character to keep you there.
John Wooden

February 10

Life isn't about waiting for the storm to pass, it's about learning how to dance in the rain.
Unknown

February 11

There are no rules, laws or traditions that apply universally including this one.
Wayne Dyer

February 12

New beginnings are often disguised as painful endings.
Lao Tsu

February 13

The biggest communication mistake is we do not listen to understand, we listen to reply.
Buddha

February 14

The past is in your head, but the future is in your hands.
Unknown

February 15

*The only time you should look back is to see
how far you've come.*
Unknown

February 16

The relationship you have with yourself
sets the tone for every other
relationship you have.
Jane Travis

February 17

Don't worry about those who talk about
you behind your back. They are behind
you for a reason.
Unknown

February 18

Never put the key to your happiness in somebody else's pocket.
Unknown

February 19

*A bad attitude is like a flat tire, you can't
go very far until you change it.*
Unknown

February 20

Get clear on whose opinions of you matter.
Brene Brown

February 21

*Focus on people who inspire you, not the
ones who annoy you.*
Buddha

February 22

*If you don't sacrifice for what you want,
what you want will be the sacrifice.*
Unknown

February 23

Speak only if it improves upon the silence.
Mahatma Gandhi

February 24

*If people throw rocks at you, collect
them and build something.
Jim Garrett*

February 25

*I cried because I had no shoes, then
I met a man who had no feet.*
Mahatma Gandhi

February 26

*Nothing can dim the light that shines
from within.*
Maya Angelou

February 27

Intellectuals solve problems, geniuses prevent them.
Albert Einstein

February 28

If you believe that feeling bad or worrying long enough will change the past or future event, then you are residing on another planet with a different reality system.
Wayne Dyer

MARCH

March 1

It's not about being the best. It's about being better than you were yesterday.
Unknown

March 2

When writing the story of your life, don't
let anyone else hold the pen.
Harley Davidson

March 3

Once you have accepted and acknowledged your flaws, no one can use them against you.
Unknown

March 4

Holding on to anger is like drinking poison and expecting the other person to die.
Unknown

March 5

*Sometime it is better to remain
silent and smile.
Buddha*

March 6

*Failure is a lesson learned; success is a
lesson applied.*
Unknown

March 7

A smart person knows what to say, a wise person knows whether to say it or not.
Unknown

March 8

Goals are Dreams with a Deadline.
Matthew Kelly

March 9

*Do not be afraid to let yourself be
guided by the Holy Spirit.*
Pope Francis

March 10

Every next level of your life will require a different version of you.
Unknown

March 11

When we're kind to ourselves, we create a reservoir of compassion that we can extend to others.
Brene Brown

March 12

*It is not because things are difficult that
we do not dare; it is because we do not dare
that things are difficult.*
Seneca

March 13

Happiness is not about getting what you want all the time. It's about loving what you have and being grateful for it.
Unknown

March 14

If years after you are grown, you think
back on your mother and your childhood
and you smile, you were raised
by a great woman.
Unknown

March 15

Be the person who cares. Be the person who makes an effort, who loves without hesitation. Be the person who makes people feel seen. There is nothing stronger than someone who continues to stay soft in a world that hasn't always been kind to them.
Unknown

March 16

Coming together is a beginning;
keeping together is progress;
working together is success.
Henry Ford

March 17

*He who does not understand your silence
will probably not understand your words.
Buddha*

March 18

You don't inspire people by being perfect;
you inspire them with how you deal with
your imperfections.
Unknown

March 19

Learn to listen. Opportunity sometimes knocks very softly.
Unknown

March 20

Your faith can move mountains and your doubts can create them.
Unknown

March 21

Be selective in your battles, because peace is sometimes better than being right.
Unknown

John Sequeira

March 22

*You are what you do, not what you
say you will do.
Unknown*

March 23

You may not control all the events that happen to you, but you can decide not to be reduced by them.
Maya Angelou

March 24

Attract what you expect; reflect what you desire; become what you respect and mirror what you admire.
Unknown

March 25

Thoughts become choices, choices become actions, actions become habits, habits become character, and your character is your destiny.
Dynamic Catholic – Decision Point

March 26

Live in such a way that if someone spoke badly of you no one would believe them.
Unknown

March 27

Be strong, but not rude; be kind but not weak; be bold but not bully; be humble but not timid; be proud but not arrogant.
Unknown

March 28

*Do something today that your future self
will thank you for.*
Unknown

March 29

*Trust takes years to build, seconds to
break and forever to repair.
Buddha*

March 30

*Continuous improvement is better
than delayed perfection.*
Mark Twain

March 31

If you don't know where you are going,
any road will take you there.
Alice in Wonderland

APRIL

April 1

A bird sitting on a branch in the tree is not afraid of the branch breaking, because her trust is not on the branch but on its own wings. Always believe in yourself.
Unknown

April 2

If you are unwilling to learn, no one can help you. If you are determined to learn, no one can stop you.
Zig Ziglar

April 3

The size of your problems is nothing compared to your ability to solve them. Don't overestimate your problems and underestimate yourself.
Buddha

April 4

Almost everything will work again if you unplug it for a few minutes, including YOU.
Anne Lamott

April 5

Courage gives us a voice and compassion gives us an ear. Without both, there is no opportunity for empathy and connection.
Brene Brown

April 6

*If you want something you've never had,
you have to do something you've
never done.
Unknown*

April 7

Don't judge yourself by your past, you don't live there anymore.
Unknown

April 8

*Accept both compliments and criticism. It
takes sunshine and rain for a
flower to grow.
Unknown*

April 9

We are all a little broken, but last time I looked broken crayons still color the same.
Unknown

John Sequeira

April 10

More people would learn from their mistakes if they weren't so busy denying them.
Unknown

April 11

If you allow people to make more withdrawals from your life than deposits, you will be in the negative and out of balance. Know when to close an account.
Unknown

April 12

When people ask, "what do you do", answer, whatever it takes! Unknown

April 13

*Forgiveness accepted heals the past,
forgiveness rejected infects the future.
Unknown*

April 14

You can have anything you want if you want it desperately enough. You must want it with an exuberance that erupts through the skin and joins the energy that created the world.
Sheila Graham

April 15

*It is in the silence of the
heart that God speaks.
Mother Teresa*

John Sequeira

April 16

*Do not learn how to react,
learn how to respond.
Buddha*

April 17

*No one can make you feel inferior
without your consent.
Eleanor Roosevelt*

April 18

*It is more probable that your attitude,
rather than your aptitude will
determine your altitude in life.*
Unknown

April 19

*The quieter you become, the
more you can hear.
Ram Dass*

April 20

There comes a time when you have to stop crossing oceans for people who wouldn't even jump puddles for you.
Unknown

April 21

Your smile is your logo; your personality is your business card; how you leave others feeling after an experience with you becomes your trademark.
Jay Danzie

April 22

Every job is a self-portrait of the person who does it. Autograph your work with excellence.
Unknown

April 23

Success at almost anything rests upon this single principle: Do the basics, do them well, and do them every day, even when you don't feel like doing them.
Matthew Kelly

April 24

*Have the maturity to know that
sometimes silence is more important
than having the last word.*
Thema Davis

April 25

Believe you can and you are halfway there.
Teddy Roosevelt

April 26

*To the mind that is still, the
whole universe surrenders.
Lao Tzu*

April 27

*A mind that opens up to a new idea
never returns to its original size.
Albert Einstein*

April 28

Every morning you have two choices,
continue to sleep with your dreams
or get up and chase them.
Unknown

April 29

Forgive others, not because they deserve forgiveness, but because you deserve peace.
Buddha

April 30

Fear is a reaction. Courage is a decision.
Winston Churchill

MAY

May 1

Too often we underestimate the power of a touch, a smile, a kind word, a listening ear, an honest compliment, or the smallest act of caring, all of which have the potential to turn a life around.
Unknown

May 2

*Each of us has a fire in our hearts
for something. It's our goal in
life to find it and keep it.
Mary Lou Retton*

May 3

God is only as far away as we place him and never as far away as we think. For it is in him that we live, move, and have our being.
Unknown

May 4

You are not alone. Within you is the infinite creative power and presence guiding you, loving you, and waiting to give you anything and everything you choose.
The Secret

May 5

*Joy is what happens to us when
we allow ourselves to recognize
how good things really are.
Marianne Williamson*

May 6

Your life doesn't get better by chance, it gets better by change.
Jim Rohn

May 7

Empathy has no script. There is no right way or wrong way to do it. It's simply listening, holding space, withholding judgment, emotionally connecting, and communicating that incredibly healing message of "You're not alone".
Brene Brown

John Sequeira

May 8

*When you finally learn your self-worth,
you stop giving others discounts.*
Unknown

May 9

If you feel like you are losing everything, remember that the trees lose their leaves every year and they still stand tall and wait for better days to come.
Unknown

May 10

You always had the power my dear;
you just had to learn it for yourself.
Glinda, the good witch of the
Wizard of Oz

May 11

*Darkness cannot drive out darkness;
only light can do that. Hate cannot
drive out hate; only love can do that.
Martin Luther King*

May 12

*Courage is the mother and father of every
great moment and movement in history.
It animates us, brings us to life, and makes
possible what has always seemed impossible.*
Matthew Kelly

May 13

*When the student is ready,
the teacher will appear.
Buddha*

May 14

*You will never reach your
destination if you stop and throw
stones at every dog that barks.
Winston Churchill*

May 15

What is to give light must endure burning.
Viktor Frankl

May 16

Live Simply. Dream big. Be grateful. Give love. Laugh lots.
Unknown

May 17

Three big lies: I am what I have. I am what I do. I am what other people say about me.
Henri Nouwen

May 18

Success is that place in the road where preparation meets opportunity.
Branch Rickey

May 19

When we are genuine with others about who we are, we invite others to do the same.
Dina Dwyer-Owens

May 20

People need love the most when they appear to deserve it least. Look around. Are you withholding warmth and compassion from someone who really needs it?
Unknown

May 21

Offering help is courageous and compassionate, but so is asking for help.
Brene Brown

John Sequeira

May 22

*A good coach can change a game. A great
coach can change a life.*
John Wooden

May 23

*When you recover or discover something
that nourishes your soul and brings
joy, care enough about yourself to
make room for it in your life.*
Jean Shinoda Bolen

May 24

Thinking is difficult. That's
why most people judge.
Carl Jung

May 25

Courage doesn't always roar. Sometimes courage is a quiet voice at the end of the day saying, I will try again tomorrow.
Mary Anne Radmacher

May 26

Don't carry your mistakes around with you. Instead, place them under your feet and use them as stepping stones to rise above them.
Unknown

May 27

Stop asking why they keep doing it and start asking why you keep allowing it.
Cathi Shaw-Marcus

May 28

May the road rise up to meet you and may the wind always be at your back.
Irish Quote

May 29

*What if everything you are going through
is preparing you for what you asked for?
Unknown*

May 30

Life is like a camera. Just focus in on what is important, capture the good times, develop from the negatives and if this doesn't work out, just take another shot.
Unknown

May 31

*In the end, only three things matter:
how much you loved, how gently
you lived and how gracefully you let
go of things not meant for you.*
Buddha

JUNE

June 1

*Focus more on the people who
inspire you rather than annoy you.
You'll get much further in life.
Kristen Butler*

June 2

*You get in life what you have
the courage to ask for.
Oprah Winfrey*

June 3

God gave you a gift of 86,400 seconds today.
Have you used one to say "Thank you"?
William Arthur Ward

June 4

If your compassion does not include yourself, it is incomplete.
Jack Kornfield

June 5

May your choices reflect your hopes, not your fears.
Unknown

June 6

Yesterday I was clever, so I wanted to change the world. Today, I'm wise, so I'm changing myself.
Rumi

June 7

Don't be pushed by your problems;
be led by your dreams.
Ralph Waldo Emerson

June 8

If you are depressed, you are living in the past. If you are anxious you are living in the future. If you are at peace, you are living in the present.
Lao Tsu

June 9

The love and attention you always thought you wanted from someone else, is the love and attention you first need to give to yourself.
Unknown

June 10

In school you are given the lesson and then the test. In life you are given the test, then the lesson.
Unknown

June 11

*A friend who understands your tears
is much more valuable than a lot of
friends who only know your smile.*
Buddha

June 12

Love all, trust a few, do wrong to none.
William Shakespeare

June 13

When things feel hectic or overwhelming,
step aside for a moment. Close your eyes
and think of three things you are grateful
for. Breathe in a sense of peace. Let go,
and start again feeling refreshed.
Unknown

June 14

When things change inside you,
things change around you.
Unknown

June 15

Be the reason someone smiles today.
Unknown

June 16

*Today I choose to be grateful for everything
I have, kind to myself and others, happy
to be alive, present, here and now!*
Unknown

June 17

A goal without a plan is just a wish.
Unknown

June 18

It's a funny thing about life, once you begin to take note of the things you are grateful for, you begin to lose sight of the things you lack.
Germany Kent

June 19

*Always remember people who have
helped you along the way, and
don't forget to lift someone up.
Roy T. Bennett*

June 20

True wealth is not measured in money or status or power. It is measured in the legacy we leave behind for those we love and those we inspire.
Cesar Chavez

June 21

*Don't give up on the person
you are becoming.
Unknown*

June 22

*Almost every successful person
begins with two beliefs: the future
can be better than the present and
I have the power to make it so.*
Unknown

June 23

*Prayer is when we direct our
thoughts to God/the Universe;
Meditation is when we listen back.*
Deepak Chopra

June 24

*To be a great listener requires patience,
focus, awareness, and most of all it
requires us to set aside our own agenda.*
Matthew Kelly

June 25

Sometimes you will never know the value of a moment until it becomes a memory.
Dr. Seuss

June 26

*You cannot go through a single day
without having an impact on the world
around you. What you do makes a
difference and you have to decide what
kind of difference you want to make.*
Jane Goodall

June 27

*Empathy is seeing with the eyes of another,
listening with the ears of another and
feeling with the heart of another.*
Alfred Alder

John Sequeira

June 28

If you light a lamp for someone else,
it will also brighten your path.
Buddha

June 29

The courage to be vulnerable is not about winning or losing; it's about the courage to show up when you can't predict or control the outcome.
Brene Brown

June 30

*Be a product of your choices not a
victim of your circumstances.*
Unknown

JULY

July 1

*Most people struggle with life balance
simply because they haven't paid the price
to decide what is really important to them.*
Stephen Covey

July 2

A gem cannot be polished without friction,
nor a person perfected without trials.
Seneca

July 3

*The cave you fear to enter holds
the treasure you seek.
Joseph Campbell*

July 4

You win a few, you lose a few.
Some get rained out. But you
got to dress for all of them.
Satchel Page

July 5

The past is a place of reference,
not a place of residence.
Unknown

July 6

Patience is when you're supposed to be mad, but you choose to understand.
Buddha

July 7

*When a flower doesn't bloom you
fix the environment in which
it grows, not the flower.*
Unknown

July 8

Live less out of habit and more out of intent.
Unknown

July 9

It's only when diverse perspectives are included, respected and valued that we can start to get a full picture of the world, who we serve, what they need, and how to successfully meet people where they are.
Brene Brown

July 10

Tough times don't last. People Do.
Julian Edelman

July 11

Coach me and I will learn;
Challenge me and I will grow;
Believe in me and I will win.
Unknown

July 12

Take your victories, whatever
they may be, cherish them, use
them, but don't settle for them.
Mia Hamm

July 13

If you're unwilling to leave someplace you've outgrown, you will never reach your full potential. To be the best, you have to constantly be challenging yourself, raising the bar, pushing the limits of what you can do. Don't stand still, leap forward.
Ronda Rousey

July 14

*Difficult roads often lead to
beautiful destinations.
Buddha*

July 15

Today I choose to live with gratitude for the love that fills my heart, the peace that rests within my spirit, and the voice of hope that says all things are possible.
Unknown

July 16

While the modern world is filling up with more and more noise, God is inviting us into the silence and into his presence. Here, in the presence of God, we will find rest for our weary hearts and minds.
Matthew Kelly

July 17

Failure to prepare is preparing to fail.
John Wooden

July 18

*Always trust your gut; it knows what
your head hasn't figured out yet.
Unknown*

July 19

*You can't go back and change the
beginning, but you can start where
you are and change the ending.
C.S. Lewis*

July 20

You can't calm the storm...so stop trying. What you can do is calm yourself. The storm will pass.
Buddha

July 21

*Be a good listener. Your ears will
never get you into trouble.*
Frank Tyger

July 22

*If you have more than three priorities,
you have no priorities. At some point,
if everything on the list is important,
then nothing is truly a driver for you.
It's just a gauzy list of feel-good words.*
Jim Collins

July 23

Forget yesterday—it has already forgotten you. Don't sweat tomorrow—you haven't even met. Instead, open your eyes and your heart to a truly precious gift—today.
Steve Maraboli

July 24

Where your talents and the needs of the world cross; there lies your vocation.
Aristotle

July 25

You don't wait to find the time for what is important. You make the time for things that matter.
Jean Case

July 26

Own the story and you get to write the ending. Deny the story and it owns you.
Brene Brown

July 27

Judge tenderly, if you must. There is usually a side you have not heard, a story you know nothing about, and a battle waged that you are not having to fight.
Traci Lea LaRussa

July 28

If you are bored with life—you don't get up every morning with a burning desire to do things—you don't have enough goals.
Lou Holtz

July 29

*Going inward. That's the real work. The
solutions are not outside of us. Get to know
who you are, because as you search for the
hero within, you inevitably become one.*
Emma Tiebens

John Sequeira

July 30

To make a difference in someone's life, you don't have to be brilliant, rich, beautiful or perfect. You just have to care.
Mandy Hale

July 31

Worrying does not empty tomorrow of its troubles, it empties today of its strength.
Corrie Ten Boom

AUGUST

August 1

When life gets too hard to stand.....kneel.
Unknown

August 2

*Dream as though you have nothing to lose.
Believe as though anything is possible. Love
as though your heart knows no bounds.
Live as though there is only today.*
Unknown

August 3

*What you become is infinitely
more important than what
you do or what you have.
Matthew Kelly*

August 4

Some people want it to happen, some wish it would happen, others make it happen.
Michael Jordan

August 5

*Forgiving doesn't make you
weak, it sets you free.
Dave Willis*

August 6

We fail the minute we let someone else define success for us. Like many of you, I spent too many years taking on projects or even positions, just to prove I could do it. It was simply accomplish-acquire-collapse-repeat.
Brene Brown

August 7

People can pressure you to do things, but the only one who makes the decision is you. Own your decisions.
Unknown

August 8

*The universe is always speaking to
us. Sending us little messages, causing
coincidences and serendipities, reminding
us to stop, to look around, to believe
in something else, something more.*
Nancy Thayer

August 9

While you were waking up today, someone else was taking their last breath. Be thankful for this day. Don't waste it.
Buddha

August 10

The most precious gift we can offer others is our presence. When mindfulness embraces those we love, they will bloom like flowers.
Thich Nhat Hanh

August 11

The most important thing in
communicating is hearing what isn't said.
Peter Drucker

John Sequeira

August 12

Kindness in words creates confidence.
Kindness in thinking creates profoundness.
Kindness in giving creates love.
Lao Tzu

August 13

Remember, the goal isn't just to finish the race of life, but to finish the race with nothing left to give.
John Wood

August 14

I've learned that people will forget
what you said, people will forget
what you did, but people will never
forget how you made them feel.
Maya Angelou

August 15

*Be kind, for everyone you meet is fighting
a battle you know nothing about.*
Wendy Mass

August 16

The real gift of gratitude is that the more grateful you are, the more present you become.
Robert Holden

August 17

Today I choose to live with gratitude for the love that fills my heart, the peace that rests within my spirit, and the voice of hope that says all things are possible.
Unknown

August 18

*What lies behind us and what
lies before us are small matters
compared to what lies within us.
Ralph Waldo Emerson*

August 19

When ego comes, everything else goes.
When ego goes, everything else comes.
Buddha

John Sequeira

August 20

No one who achieves success does so without the help of others. The wise and confident acknowledge this help with gratitude.
Alfred North Whitehead

August 21

The great thing in this world is not so much where you stand but in what direction are you moving.
Oliver Wendell Holmes

August 22

I'm thankful for my struggle because without it I wouldn't have stumbled across my strength.
Unknown

August 23

Spread love everywhere you go. Let no one ever come to you without leaving happier.
Mother Teresa

August 24

When one door of happiness closes,
another opens, but often we look so long
at the closed door that we do not see
the one that has been opened for us.
Helen Keller

August 25

There is no exercise better for the heart than reaching down and lifting people up.
John Holmes

August 26

Many Big Bets were executed because someone boldly envisioned a different future—one not yet seen by others—and pursued it. What kind of world do you want to see? What kind of future do you want to build? The key is tuning out those who don't share your vision and persevering toward your goal.
Jean Case

August 27

Weak people revenge, strong people forgive, intelligent people ignore.
Buddha

John Sequeira

August 28

Go out on a limb. That's where the fruit is.
Jimmy Carter

August 29

It's your road and yours alone.
Others may walk it with you, but
no one can walk it for you.
Rumi

John Sequeira

August 30

The best time to plant a tree was twenty years ago; the next best time is now.
Proverb

August 31

Never doubt that a small group of
thoughtful people could change the world.
Indeed, it's the only thing that has.
Margaret Mead

SEPTEMBER

September 1

If there are pieces of your past that are weighing you down, it's time to leave them behind. You are not what has happened to you. You are someone unimaginably greater than you have ever considered, and maybe it's time to consider all the possibilities that are within you.
Matthew Kelly

John Sequeira

September 2

Setting boundaries is making clear what's okay and what's not okay and why.
Brene Brown

September 3

*Luck is what happens when
preparation meets opportunity.*
Seneca

September 4

*Our days are happier when we give
people a bit of our heart rather
than a piece of our mind.*
Unknown

September 5

*May your choices reflect your
hopes, not your fears.*
Nelson Mandela

September 6

Ultimately, peace is the fruit of knowing that you are spending your life on a worthy purpose—that each day you are able to love more than the day before, that you are becoming a better person, that you are responding to the gentle whisper of God calling you to inspire and improve the lives of others.
Unknown

September 7

Worry never robs tomorrow of its sorrow. It only saps today of its joy.
Leo Buscaglia

September 8

*Some of your greatest blessings
come with patience.*
Buddha

September 9

*Our Lives begin to end the day we become
silent about the things that matter.
Martin Luther King*

September 10

My mission in life is not merely to survive, but to thrive; and to do so with some passion, some compassion, some humor, and some style.
Maya Angelou

September 11

Rather than being your thoughts and emotions, be the awareness behind them.
Eckhart Tolle

September 12

You don't have to control your thoughts, you just have to stop letting them control you.
Dan Millman

September 13

How you make others feel about themselves says a lot about you.
Unknown

September 14

Forget what hurt you, but never forget what it taught you.
Shannon L. Alder

September 15

Letting go doesn't mean forgetting,
it just means we stop carrying the
energy of the past into the present.
Yung Pueblo

John Sequeira

September 16

*Ten years from now you want to be able to
say you chose this life, not settled for it.
Unknown*

September 17

Sometimes when you are in a dark place you think you've been buried, but actually, you've been planted.
Christine Caine

September 18

The bad news is nothing lasts forever.
The good news is nothing lasts forever.
J. Cole

September 19

*With awareness, we can make conscious
choices, instead of letting our habitual
thoughts and patterns run the show.*
Tamara Levitt

September 20

*It's not about perfect. It's about effort.
And when you bring that effort every
single day that's where transformation
happens. That's how change occurs.
Jillian Michaels*

September 21

*Don't quit yet, the worst moments
are usually followed by the most
beautiful silver linings. You just have
to stay strong, remember to keep
your head up and remain hopeful.*
Unknown

September 22

Don't be afraid to start over again. This time you're not starting from scratch, you're starting from experience.
Unknown

September 23

*Never explain yourself, your real
friends don't need it, and your
enemies won't believe it.
Buddha*

John Sequeira

September 24

*I alone can't change the world,
but I can cast a stone across the
waters to create new ripples.*
Mother Theresa

September 25

Be a rainbow in someone's cloud.
John Quincy Adams

September 26

Always remember to fall asleep with a dream and wake up with a purpose.
Unknown

September 27

Personally, I'm always ready to learn,
although I do not always like being taught.
Winston Churchill

September 28

*Your past does not determine who you are;
it prepares you for who you will become.*
Unknown

September 29

*When we let freedom ring, when we let it
ring from every village and every hamlet,
from every state and every city, we will
be able to speed up that day when all
of God's children, black men and white
men, Jews and Gentiles, Protestants
and Catholics, will be able to join hands
and sing in the words of that old Negro
spiritual, Free at last! Free at last! Thank
God Almighty, we are free at last!
Martin Luther King*

John Sequeira

September 30

*You cannot shake hands
with a clenched fist.
Golda Meir*

OCTOBER

October 1

*As I grow older, I pay less attention to
what people say. I just watch what they do.*
Andrew Carnegie

October 2

If passion drives you, let reason hold the reins.
Ben Franklin

October 3

*I am a little pencil in the hand
of a writing God who is sending
a love letter to the world.*
Mother Teresa

October 4

*If you want to gather honey,
don't kick over the beehive.
Dale Carnegie*

October 5

If you stumble make it part of the dance.
Unknown

October 6

Talk to yourself the way you would talk to someone you love.
Brene Brown

October 7

*Be more concerned with your
character than with your reputation.
Your character is what you really
are while your reputation is merely
what others think you are.
John Wooden*

October 8

*Whether you think you can or think
you can't –you are correct.
Henry Ford*

October 9

A person cannot discover new oceans until they have the courage to lose sight of the shore.
Unknown

October 10

Silence is the best reply to a fool.
Buddha

October 11

You must learn to master a new way to think before you can master a new way to be.
Unknown

John Sequeira

October 12

*Don't wait for the -perfect moment.
Take the moment and make it perfect.
Unknown*

October 13

*Stop planting flowers in people's yard
who aren't going to water them.
Unknown*

October 14

I knew that if I failed, I wouldn't regret that. But I knew the one thing I might regret is not trying.
Jeff Bezos

October 15

Face your fears, by creating a plan. We are usually afraid of the unknown, so expose it, plan it and conquer your fears.
Unknown

October 16

Keep working, even when
no one is watching.
Alex Morgan

October 17

Happiness is not something you postpone for the future. It is something you design for the present.
Unknown

October 18

A coach is someone who tells you what you don't want to hear, who has you see what you don't want to see, so you can be who you have always known you could be.
Tom Landry

October 19

*There is a calmness to a life lived
in gratitude, a quiet joy.*
Unknown

October 20

Between stimulus and response, there is a space. In that space is our power to choose our response. In our response lies our growth and our freedom.
Viktor Frankl

October 21

*Speak only if you feel your words
are better than the silence.*
Buddha

October 22

You are off to great places! Today is your day. Your mountain is waiting, so.....get on your way!
Dr. Seuss

October 23

Happiness does not depend on accumulating more things, but on the mindset we have concerning the things we already do possess.
Fulton Sheen

October 24

*One of the happiest moments in life
is when you find the courage to let
go of what you can't change.*
Unknown

October 25

If a man knows not to which port
he sails, no wind is favorable.
Seneca

October 26

Today, I choose to live with gratitude for the love that fills my heart, the peace that rests within my spirit, and the voice of hope that says all things are possible.
Unknown

October 27

*People lose their way when
they lose their why.
Unknown*

October 28

Rule number one is, don't sweat the small stuff. Rule number two is, it's all small stuff.
Jack Kornfield

October 29

*In the end only three things matter:
How much you loved, how gently you
lived, and how gracefully you let go
of the things not meant for you.*
Unknown

John Sequeira

October 30

*Do not follow where the path may
lead. Go instead where there is
no path and leave a trail.*
Muriel Strode

October 31

*Making mistakes is better
than faking perfections.
Unknown*

NOVEMBER

November 1

Every person in this life has something to teach me—and as soon as I accept that, I open myself up to truly listening.
Catherine Doucette

November 2

Don't do something permanently stupid because you are temporarily upset.
Unknown

November 3

We're scared to have hard conversations because we can't control the path or outcome and we start coming out of our skin when we don't get to resolution fast enough. It's as if we'd rather have a bad solution that leads to action than stay in the uncertainty of problem identification.
Brene Brown

John Sequeira

November 4

*Control your own destiny
or someone else will.*
Jack Welch

November 5

*The 3 C's of life: You must make
the Choice to take the Chance, if
you want anything to Change.
Unknown*

November 6

Hatred corrodes the container
it is carried in.
Unknown

November 7

Unforgiveness tortures the person who harbors it. Forgiveness won't make the offense all right; it will make YOU all right. If you forgive, you do not carry the weight of a negative experience.
Beth Moore

November 8

God invites you to experience the power of little things. If you cannot find peace in the journey, you will never find peace in the destination. Be present in your own life.
Unknown

November 9

*One of the happiest moments in life
is when you find the courage to let
go of what you can't change.*
Unknown

November 10

*Don't ask yourself what the world needs;
ask yourself what makes you come alive.
And then go and do that. Because what the
world needs is people who have come alive.
Howard Washington Thurman*

November 11

When everything seems to be going against you, remember that the airplane takes off against the wind, not with it.
Henry Ford

John Sequeira

November 12

*Yesterday is history, tomorrow is
a mystery, but today is a gift. That
is why it is called the present.*
Unknown

November 13

If you want to change your life, change your choices.
Unknown

November 14

Allow simplicity to direct your life, and permit a measure of silence and solitude to have their proper place in the course of your daily activities. Then you will catch glimpses of the best version of yourself.
Matthew Kelly

November 15

Don't close the book when bad things happen in your life, just turn the page and begin a new chapter.
Unknown

November 16

When an archer misses the mark, he turns and looks for the fault within himself. Failure to hit the bull's eye is never the fault of the target. To improve your aim, improve yourself.
By Gilbert Arland

November 17

The richest wealth is wisdom.
The strongest weapon is patience.
The best security is faith.
Buddha

November 18

My cup is always half full.
Unknown

November 19

*Don't fear failure so much that you refuse
to try new things. The saddest summary
of life contains three descriptions: could
have, might have and should have.*
Louis E. Boone

November 20

*People don't care how much you know
until they know how much you care.
Brene Brown*

November 21

*Don't measure your progress
by someone else's ruler.
Unknown*

John Sequeira

November 22

The secret to living well and longer
is, eat half, walk double, laugh triple
and love without measure.
Tibetan Proverb

November 23

*Life is about accepting the challenges
along the way, choosing to keep moving
forward and savoring the journey.*
Roy T. Bennett

John Sequeira

November 24

Progress is being aware when there is a storm happening inside of you and remaining calm as it passes by.
Yung Pueblo

November 25

Courage doesn't mean you don't get afraid. Courage means you don't let the fear stop you.
Bethany Hamilton

November 26

I am not a product of my circumstances.
I am a product of my decisions.
Stephen Covey

November 27

*Follow your heart, but take
your brain with you.
Buddha*

November 28

First do what is necessary, then do what is possible, and before long you will find yourself doing the impossible.
St. Francis of Assisi

November 29

Emotional maturity doesn't come with
age, it comes from self-awareness.
Tory Eletto

November 30

Patience takes root, when we learn
to love people just as they are, not as
we want them to be. Patience accepts
the other person even when he or she
acts differently than I would like.
Christopher West

DECEMBER

December 1

At the end of the day, the only questions I will ask myself are: Did I love enough? Did I laugh enough? Did I make a difference?
Unknown

December 2

Don't run away from heavy emotions,
honor the anger, give pain the space it
needs to breathe-this is how you let go.
Yung Pueblo

December 3

A soft reminder; not everything that weighs you down is yours to carry.
Unknown

December 4

When thinking about life, remember this: No amount of guilt can change the past and no amount of anxiety can change the future.
Unknown

December 5

Forget who hurt you yesterday, but don't forget those who love you every day. Forget the past that makes you cry and focus on the present that makes you smile. Forget the pain, but never the lessons you gained.
Buddha

December 6

Worrying does not take away tomorrow's troubles. It takes away today's peace.
Unknown

December 7

*Until you make the unconscious
conscious, it will direct your life
and you will call it fate.
Carl Jung*

December 8

*Not all storms come to disrupt your
life; some come to clear your path.
Unknown*

December 9

*If you are neutral in situations of injustice,
you have chosen the side of the oppressor.*
Desmond Tutu

December 10

The Universe is not outside of you.
Look inside yourself; everything
that you want, you already are.
Rumi

December 11

Do things for people not because of who they are or what they do in return, but because of who you are.
Harold Kushner

December 12

*If you believe it will work out, you'll
see opportunities. If you believe
it won't, you'll see obstacles.*
Wayne Dyer

December 13

I can accept failure, everyone fails at something. But I can't accept not trying.
Michael Jordan

December 14

Helping one person might not change the world but it could change the world for one person.
Buddha

December 15

Empathy is at the heart of connection-it is the circuit board for leaning into the feelings of others, reflecting back a shared experience of the world, and reminding them that they are not alone.
Brene Brown

John Sequeira

December 16

Our prime purpose in this life is to help others. And if you can't help them, at least don't hurt them.
Dalai Lama

December 17

Happiness is when what you think, what you say, and what you do are in harmony.
Mahatma Gandhi

December 18

*One of the hardest things to learn
in life is which bridges to cross
and which bridges to burn.
Oprah Winfrey*

December 19

Being humble means recognizing that we are not on earth to see how important we can become, but to see how much difference we can make in the lives of others.
Gordon Hinckley

December 20

People fail to get along because they fear each other; they fear each other because they don't know each other; they don't know each other because they have not communicated with each other.
Martin Luther King

December 21

*When obstacles arise, you change your
direction to reach your goal; you do not
change your decision to get there.*
Zig Ziglar

December 22

*Let gratitude be the pillow upon which
you kneel to say your nightly prayer.
And let faith be the bridge you build
to overcome evil and welcome good.
Maya Angelou*

December 23

Open your heart, open your mind,
open your soul to the miracles God
wants to work in and through you.
Matthew Kelly

December 24

*Never stop learning, because
life never stops teaching.
Buddha*

December 25

Today I choose to live with gratitude for the love that fills my heart, the peace that rests within my spirit, and the voice of hope that says all things are possible.
Unknown

December 26

If thy think your dreams are crazy,
show them what crazy dreams can do.
Serena Williams

December 27

Wear gratitude like a cloak, and it will feed every corner of your life.
Rumi

December 28

Sometimes the bad things that happen in our lives put us directly on the path to the best things that will ever happen to us.
Nicole Reed

December 29

*What we know matters but
who we are matters more.
Brene Brown*

John Sequeira

December 30

Today may we choose peace over chaos, respect over belittling, thoughtfulness over reaction, faith over fear and others over ourselves.
Mark Charles

December 31

My goal is not to be better than anyone else, but to better than I used to be.
Buddha

Made in the USA
Monee, IL
28 December 2020

55819961R00223